Adult ADHD tool

Dickson Williams

Table of content

Introduction to ADHD

In the dynamic tapestry of human experience, there exists a spectrum of minds, each weaving its own intricate pattern. Amidst this diversity, Attention Deficit Hyperactivity Disorder (ADHD) emerges as a thread that shapes the lives of many individuals. Far from a mere diagnosis, ADHD is a nuanced aspect of the human psyche that influences the way one navigates the world.

ADHD is not a sign of weakness, but a manifestation of a unique cognitive landscape. It brings with it a distinctive set of strengths, challenges, and untapped potentials. This book seeks to unravel the layers of understanding surrounding Adult ADHD, offering a comprehensive toolkit designed to empower, guide, and illuminate the journey toward not just coping, but thriving.

As we embark on this exploration, let us cast aside preconceived notions and embark on a journey of discovery. Within these pages, we will navigate the intricacies of ADHD, celebrating the strengths it bestows, addressing the challenges it presents, and equipping individuals with the tools they need to forge a path toward fulfillment and success. Together, let us embrace the vibrant tapestry of ADHD and harness its unique colors to create a life that is not only understood but truly lived.

Chapter 1:What is ADHD?

ADHD stands for Attention Deficit Hyperactivity Disorder. It is a neurodevelopmental disorder that affects both children and adults. ADHD is characterized by persistent patterns of inattention, hyperactivity, and impulsivity that can impact daily functioning and quality of life.

Key Features of ADHD:

1. Inattention:
   - Individuals with ADHD may struggle with sustaining attention on tasks, frequently make careless mistakes, and have difficulty organizing activities.

2. Hyperactivity:
   - Hyperactivity in ADHD often presents as excessive fidgeting, restlessness, and difficulty remaining seated in situations where it is expected.

3. Impulsivity:
   - Impulsivity manifests as hasty decision-making, difficulty waiting one's turn, and a tendency to interrupt others.

4. Subtypes: ADHD is categorized into three subtypes: Predominantly Inattentive Presentation, Predominantly Hyperactive-Impulsive Presentation, and Combined Presentation, which includes symptoms of both inattention and hyperactivity-impulsivity.

5. Onset and Duration:Symptoms of ADHD typically appear in childhood, and the condition can persist into adolescence and adulthood. Some individuals may be diagnosed later in life.

6. Impact on Daily Functioning: ADHD can affect various aspects of life, including academic and occupational performance, relationships, and overall well-being.

7.Coexisting Conditions:ADHD often coexists with other conditions, such as learning disabilities, anxiety, depression, and sleep disorders.

8. Diagnosis and Treatment:Diagnosis involves a comprehensive evaluation by a healthcare professional, considering the presence of symptoms across different settings. Treatment approaches may include behavioral interventions, psychoeducation, and, in some cases, medication.

It's important to note that ADHD is a neurobiological condition, and individuals with ADHD often have unique strengths and talents. While it poses challenges, with appropriate support and management, individuals with ADHD can lead fulfilling and successful lives. Diagnosis and intervention tailored to the individual's specific needs are crucial for effective management.

Adult ADHD, or attention-deficit/hyperactivity disorder in adults, is typically categorized into three main types, based on the predominant symptoms:

1. ADHD, Predominantly Inattentive Presentation:
   - Individuals with this type primarily struggle with attention and organization.
   - Common symptoms include difficulty sustaining attention, forgetfulness, trouble organizing tasks, and a tendency to avoid or procrastinate on tasks requiring sustained mental effort.

2. ADHD, Predominantly Hyperactive-Impulsive Presentation:

- This type is characterized by hyperactivity and impulsivity without significant inattention.
   - Symptoms may include restlessness, impulsive decision-making, difficulty waiting one's turn, and a tendency to interrupt others.

3. ADHD, Combined Presentation:
   - This is the most common type, where individuals experience a combination of both inattentive and hyperactive-impulsive symptoms.
   - Symptoms include a mix of attention difficulties, hyperactivity, and impulsivity.

It's important to note that ADHD symptoms can vary widely among individuals, and some people may exhibit a combination of features from different presentations. Additionally, adults with ADHD often face challenges such as difficulty with time management, organization, and maintaining relationships.

Diagnosing adult ADHD involves a comprehensive evaluation by a healthcare professional, considering the individual's history, symptoms, and their impact on daily functioning. Treatment may involve a combination of behavioral interventions, psychoeducation, and, in some cases, medication. It's crucial for individuals experiencing symptoms of ADHD to seek professional assessment and guidance for appropriate management.

Causes of adult ADHD

The exact causes of adult ADHD (attention-deficit/hyperactivity disorder) are not fully understood, and it is likely to be influenced by a combination of genetic, neurological, environmental, and developmental factors. Here are some key factors that may contribute to the development of adult ADHD:

1. Genetics:

- There is a strong genetic component to ADHD. Individuals with a family history of ADHD are more likely to have the disorder themselves. Specific genes related to neurotransmitter function and brain development are thought to play a role.

2. Neurobiological Factors:
   - Differences in brain structure and function have been observed in individuals with ADHD. Irregularities in certain neurotransmitters (such as dopamine and norepinephrine) and their receptors are believed to contribute to the symptoms of ADHD.

3. Prenatal and Perinatal Factors:
   - Exposure to certain prenatal and perinatal factors may increase the risk of ADHD. These factors include premature birth, low birth weight, and exposure to tobacco smoke, alcohol, or drugs during pregnancy.

4. Environmental Factors:
   - Certain environmental factors may contribute to the development of ADHD. Exposure to lead or other environmental toxins during early childhood has been studied in relation to ADHD risk.

5. Brain Injury:
   - Traumatic brain injury or damage to the brain during early development can be a contributing factor. Injury to the frontal lobes, which are associated with executive functions, attention, and impulse control, may increase the risk of ADHD.

6. Developmental Factors:
   - Delays or disruptions in early development, particularly in the areas of attention and impulse control, may contribute to the development of ADHD.

7. Psychosocial Factors:

- While not a direct cause, certain psychosocial factors can exacerbate symptoms or contribute to the challenges associated with ADHD. These may include high levels of stress, chaotic family environments, or inconsistent parenting.

It's important to note that ADHD is a complex and heterogeneous disorder, and the interplay of various factors can differ among individuals. Additionally, not everyone with risk factors will develop ADHD, and not all individuals with ADHD will share the same set of contributing factors. Diagnosis and understanding of ADHD are typically based on a comprehensive evaluation by healthcare professionals, considering various aspects of an individual's history and symptoms.

Signs and Symptoms of ADHD in Adults

The following are Signs and Symptoms of ADHD in Adults:

1. Difficulty Sustaining Attention:
   - Adults with ADHD may struggle to maintain focus on tasks, leading to difficulty completing work assignments or engaging in conversations.

2. Forgetfulness:Forgetfulness is common, including forgetting appointments, deadlines, or where personal items were placed.

3. Impulsivity:Adults with ADHD may act impulsively, making decisions without fully considering the consequences. This can manifest in both personal and professional contexts.

4. Poor Time Management:Difficulty managing time effectively, leading to chronic lateness, missed deadlines, and a sense of being overwhelmed by responsibilities.

5. Procrastination: Procrastination is a common challenge, with individuals delaying tasks until the last minute due to difficulty initiating and sustaining effort.

6. Restlessness and Hyperactivity:While hyperactivity may decrease in adulthood, restlessness, and an internal sense of being "on the go" persist. Adults with ADHD may have difficulty relaxing.

7. Difficulty Organizing Tasks:Challenges in organizing tasks and activities, both at work and in daily life. This includes problems with prioritization and planning.

8. Impaired Executive Functioning: Executive functions, such as problem-solving, decision-making, and goal-setting, may be impaired in adults with ADHD.

9. Difficulty Listening in Conversations: Adults with ADHD may find it challenging to listen attentively in conversations, leading to misunderstandings or missed details.

10. Frequent Mood Swings:Mood swings and emotional dysregulation can be present, with individuals experiencing intense emotions that may fluctuate rapidly.

11. Relationship Challenges:Difficulties in maintaining relationships due to communication issues, forgetfulness, and impulsivity. Relationship patterns may include a history of instability.

12. Job Instability:Adults with ADHD may experience difficulties in maintaining consistent employment due to challenges such as poor time management and difficulty adhering to routines.

13. Substance Abuse Risk: There is an increased risk of substance abuse in individuals with ADHD, as some may use substances as a coping mechanism for managing symptoms.

14. Low Self-Esteem: Struggles with self-esteem and feelings of underachievement are common, particularly if ADHD symptoms have impacted academic and professional achievements.

15. Difficulty with Details: Adults with ADHD may have difficulty managing and attending to details in tasks, leading to errors and oversights.

Effects of Adult ADD/ADHD

The following are some of the effects of adult ADHD

1. Impact on Work Performance:Adults with ADHD may experience challenges in maintaining consistent work performance, including difficulties with time management, organization, and task completion.

2. Relationship Strain:ADHD can contribute to difficulties in relationships, as symptoms like forgetfulness, impulsivity, and inattention may lead to misunderstandings and conflicts.

3. Educational and Career Challenges:Individuals with adult ADHD may face challenges in educational pursuits and career advancement, impacting their ability to reach their full potential.

4. Low Self-Esteem:Struggles with ADHD-related difficulties can contribute to low self-esteem, especially if individuals face criticism or negative feedback related to their symptoms.

5. Financial Difficulties:Impulsivity and challenges in planning may lead to financial difficulties, including impulsive spending and poor financial management.

6. Increased Risk of Accidents:Adults with ADHD may be at a higher risk of accidents and injuries due to impulsivity, distractibility, and difficulty with risk assessment.

7. Mental Health Co-occurring Conditions:ADHD often coexists with other mental health conditions such as anxiety, depression, and substance use disorders, further impacting overall well-being.

8. Chronic Stress:Managing the demands of daily life with ADHD can contribute to chronic stress, affecting physical health and exacerbating symptoms.

9. Sleep Disorders:Adults with ADHD may be prone to sleep difficulties, including insomnia, which can further impact their ability to focus and function during the day.

10. Social Isolation:ADHD-related challenges in communication and maintaining attention during social interactions may contribute to social isolation and difficulties in forming and maintaining friendships.

11. Legal Issues: Impulsivity and difficulties with impulse control may lead to legal issues, such as traffic violations or impulsive decision-making that has legal consequences.

12. Health Neglect: Adults with ADHD may neglect their health, such as missing medical appointments or not adhering to recommended health practices, due to difficulties with organization and follow-through.

13. Difficulty with Household Responsibilities: Managing household responsibilities, such as cleaning and organizing, can be challenging for adults with ADHD, impacting daily living.

14. Coping Mechanisms and Substance Use:Some individuals with ADHD may develop maladaptive coping mechanisms, including substance use, to manage symptoms or alleviate stress.

15.Relationship Struggles:Relationship dynamics may be strained due to ADHD-related challenges, including communication difficulties, impulsivity, and inconsistent focus on personal relationships.

It's crucial to recognize that while ADHD can present challenges, individuals with ADHD also often demonstrate unique strengths and talents. With appropriate support, strategies, and interventions, individuals with adult ADHD can effectively manage their symptoms and lead fulfilling lives. Seeking professional guidance for diagnosis and tailored treatment plans is essential for effective management.

Treatment for Adult ADHD:

1. Medication:Stimulant Medications:Commonly prescribed stimulants include methylphenidate (e.g., Ritalin) and amphetamine-based medications (e.g., Adderall). These can help improve attention and focus.
Non-Stimulant Medications: Atomoxetine (Strattera) and guanfacine (Intuniv) are non-stimulant options that may be prescribed, particularly if stimulants are not well-tolerated.

2. Behavioral Therapy:

Cognitive Behavioral Therapy (CBT):CBT can help individuals with ADHD develop coping strategies, improve time management, and address negative thought patterns.

-Psychoeducation: Learning about ADHD and its management can empower individuals to understand and address their symptoms effectively.

3. Organization and Time Management Strategies:Developing practical strategies for organization and time management is crucial. This may include using planners, setting reminders, and breaking tasks into smaller, manageable steps.

4. Coaching and Support Groups:ADHD coaching provides personalized support and strategies for managing daily challenges. Support groups allow individuals to share experiences and learn from others facing similar issues.

5. Lifestyle Modifications: Regular Exercise:Physical activity can help regulate mood, improve focus, and manage stress.
- Healthy Nutrition:A balanced diet with regular meals can contribute to stable energy levels and overall well-being.
- Adequate Sleep: Establishing a consistent sleep routine is essential for managing ADHD symptoms.

6. Mindfulness and Relaxation Techniques:
Practices such as mindfulness meditation, deep breathing exercises, and yoga can help manage stress and improve focus.

7. Environmental Modifications: Structuring the environment to minimize distractions and create an organized space can assist individuals with ADHD in staying focused.

8. Social Skills Training: For those facing challenges in interpersonal relationships, social skills training can provide strategies for effective communication and relationship building.

9. Workplace Accommodations: Discussing ADHD with employers and implementing workplace accommodations, such as flexible schedules or task modifications, can support success in the workplace.

10. Medication Management: Regular monitoring and adjustment of medication under the guidance of a healthcare professional to ensure optimal effectiveness and manage potential side effects.

11. Continued Education: Continuous education about ADHD and its management, staying informed about new strategies and treatments, and remaining engaged in one's own care.

12. Family Support and Education: Involving family members in understanding ADHD and its impact, fostering a supportive environment, and providing practical assistance when needed.

Treatment for adult ADHD is often individualized, considering the specific needs and preferences of each person. A comprehensive approach that combines medication, behavioral interventions, and lifestyle modifications can be highly effective in managing symptoms and improving overall functioning. Seeking guidance from healthcare professionals, including psychiatrists, psychologists, and ADHD specialists, is essential for developing a tailored treatment plan.

Health disparities related to adult ADHD can manifest in various ways, often stemming from a combination of societal, economic, and healthcare factors. Some key aspects of health disparities in adult ADHD include:

1. Underdiagnosis and Misdiagnosis:
Adults with ADHD may be underdiagnosed or misdiagnosed, leading to delayed or inadequate treatment. Lack of awareness among healthcare professionals and societal stigma can contribute to this issue.

2. Access to Healthcare:
Disparities in access to healthcare services can impact individuals with ADHD. Those without adequate health insurance or limited access to mental health professionals may face challenges in receiving timely and comprehensive care.

3. Socioeconomic Factors:
Socioeconomic status can influence the likelihood of receiving a timely ADHD diagnosis and accessing appropriate treatment. Individuals with lower socioeconomic status may face additional barriers, including limited access to mental health resources.

4. Educational Disparities:
ADHD often intersects with educational challenges. Adults with ADHD may face difficulties in academic and occupational settings, affecting their career opportunities and overall well-being.

5. Cultural Sensitivity:
Cultural factors can play a significant role in the recognition and acceptance of ADHD. Different cultural norms and beliefs may influence how ADHD symptoms are perceived, diagnosed, and treated within various communities.

6. Stigma and Discrimination:

Stigma surrounding mental health issues, including ADHD, can lead
to discrimination and reluctance to seek help. Addressing societal
attitudes toward mental health is crucial in reducing disparities.

7. Gender Differences:
ADHD is often diagnosed less frequently in females, and symptoms
may manifest differently. This gender bias can result in delayed or
overlooked diagnoses in women, impacting their ability to access
appropriate interventions.

8. Coexisting Conditions:
Individuals with ADHD frequently have coexisting conditions, such
as anxiety or depression. Disparities in mental health support and
treatment can exacerbate the challenges faced by those with comorbid
conditions.

9. Criminal Justice System Involvement:
There is a higher prevalence of individuals with ADHD in the
criminal justice system. Addressing this issue requires a holistic
approach that considers mental health treatment alternatives to
incarceration.

Addressing these health disparities requires a multifaceted approach
that includes increased awareness, education, improved access to
mental health services, and efforts to reduce stigma surrounding
mental health conditions. Advocacy for inclusive healthcare policies
and greater cultural competence within the healthcare system is
essential to promote equity for adults with ADHD.

Chapter 2: Understanding Adult ADHD

Attention Deficit Hyperactivity Disorder (ADHD) is not confined to the realm of childhood; it persists into adulthood, shaping the experiences and perceptions of those who carry its imprint. At its core, Adult ADHD is a neurodevelopmental condition that affects executive functions, such as attention, impulse control, and organization.

1. A Continuum of Attention:
   ADHD manifests along a spectrum, leading to variations in how it impacts individuals. While attention challenges are central, some may struggle with hyperactivity, impulsivity, or a combination of these traits.

2. The Brain's Unique Wiring: Neurologically, ADHD is characterized by differences in brain structure and function. Dopamine, a neurotransmitter, plays a pivotal role, influencing attention and reward systems. Understanding these neurological nuances is key to comprehending the diverse facets of Adult ADHD.

3. Lifelong Impact: Contrary to earlier beliefs, ADHD doesn't magically vanish with the transition to adulthood. Instead, its influence adapts, presenting distinct challenges in academic, professional, and personal spheres. Recognizing these persistent effects is crucial for effective management.

4. Beyond the Stereotypes: Dispelling stereotypes is essential in understanding Adult ADHD. It's not merely a lack of focus but a

complex interplay of cognitive processes. Many individuals with ADHD also possess remarkable creativity, energy, and resilience.

5. Coexisting Conditions: Adult ADHD often coexists with other mental health conditions, such as anxiety or depression. Untangling these overlapping threads is vital for a holistic approach to well-being.

By delving into the intricacies of Adult ADHD, we lay the foundation for a more empathetic and informed perspective. This understanding forms the bedrock upon which we can build a toolkit for navigating the unique challenges and harnessing the strengths inherent in the ADHD experience.

The epidemiology of adult

The epidemiology of adult ADHD involves studying the prevalence, distribution, and factors influencing the occurrence of Attention-Deficit/Hyperactivity Disorder in the adult population. Here are key points related to adult ADHD epidemiology:

1. Prevalence:
   The prevalence of ADHD tends to persist into adulthood for a significant portion of individuals who had the disorder in childhood. Estimates suggest that approximately 2.5% to 5% of adults worldwide may have ADHD.

2. Gender Differences:
   ADHD is often diagnosed more frequently in males during childhood, but in adulthood, the gender gap narrows. Research indicates that ADHD may be underdiagnosed in females, as their symptoms can manifest differently.

3. Persistence from Childhood:

Many adults with ADHD continue to experience symptoms that originated in childhood. However, some individuals may not receive a diagnosis until adulthood, particularly if their symptoms were not recognized earlier.

4. Late-Onset ADHD:
While ADHD often begins in childhood, there is recognition of late-onset ADHD, where symptoms emerge for the first time in adulthood. Late-onset cases may be associated with unique challenges and considerations.

5. Comorbidity:
ADHD frequently coexists with other mental health conditions in adults. Common comorbidities include anxiety disorders, mood disorders (such as depression), substance use disorders, and personality disorders.

6. Impact on Daily Functioning:
ADHD can significantly impact various aspects of adult life, including academic and occupational functioning, relationships, and overall quality of life.

7. Educational and Occupational Implications:
Adults with ADHD may face challenges in educational and occupational settings. Difficulties with attention, organization, and time management can affect academic and work performance.

8. Quality of Life:
Individuals with adult ADHD may experience impairments in their quality of life. These can stem from difficulties in maintaining relationships, managing responsibilities, and coping with associated mental health conditions.

9.   Diagnostic Challenges:
Diagnosing ADHD in adults can be challenging due to factors such as the misconception that ADHD is exclusively a childhood disorder. Adults may present with more subtle symptoms that differ from those seen in children.

10.   Global Variances:
ADHD prevalence rates can vary across different regions and cultures. Factors such as awareness, cultural perceptions of mental health, and diagnostic practices contribute to these variations.

Understanding the epidemiology of adult ADHD is crucial for developing effective public health policies, educational initiatives, and healthcare strategies to support individuals living with the condition. As research in this area continues, it enhances our understanding of the diverse presentations and challenges associated with adult ADHD.

The prognosis for adults ADHD

The prognosis for adults with ADHD can vary based on individual factors, including the severity of symptoms, the presence of comorbid conditions, and the effectiveness of treatment strategies. Here are some key points regarding the prognosis of adult ADHD:

1.   Improvement with Age:
In many cases, symptoms of ADHD may improve with age. As individuals develop coping strategies and life skills, they often find better ways to manage their symptoms.

2.   Lifelong Challenges:
While some individuals experience a reduction in symptoms over time, others continue to face challenges associated with ADHD throughout their lives. The persistence of symptoms can vary widely.

3.   Effectiveness of Treatment:

The prognosis is influenced by the effectiveness of treatment. Individuals who receive appropriate interventions, including behavioral therapy, medication, and support, may experience significant improvement in symptoms and daily functioning.

4. Comorbidity Impact:
The presence of comorbid conditions, such as anxiety or depression, can influence the overall prognosis. Addressing these coexisting conditions is often crucial for a more positive outcome.

5. Educational and Occupational Success:
With the right support and accommodations, adults with ADHD can achieve success in both educational and occupational settings. Strategies such as time management, organization, and effective communication play key roles.

6. Relationships and Social Functioning:
ADHD can impact interpersonal relationships and social functioning. Developing strong communication skills, fostering understanding among family and friends, and seeking support can contribute to positive relationship outcomes.

7. Continued Self-Management:
Successful management of adult ADHD often requires ongoing self-awareness and self-management. This may involve utilizing coping strategies, staying organized, and adapting to changing life circumstances.

8. Impact on Quality of Life:
The overall impact of ADHD on an individual's quality of life is a significant consideration. Through a combination of treatment, self-awareness, and support, many individuals with ADHD can lead fulfilling lives.

9.   Career Paths and Stability:
  ADHD can affect career choices and stability. However, with
appropriate accommodations, supportive work environments, and
tailored strategies, individuals with ADHD can find success in various
professions.

10.   Continued Research and Understanding:
  Ongoing research contributes to a better understanding of adult
ADHD, leading to improved diagnostic tools, treatment options, and
support strategies. This evolving knowledge may positively influence
the long-term prognosis for individuals with ADHD.

It's essential for individuals with adult ADHD to work collaboratively
with healthcare professionals to develop and adjust treatment plans as
needed. Additionally, building a support network and seeking
resources within the community can enhance the overall prognosis
and quality of life.

Define Adult ADHD and dispel common myths

Adult Attention Deficit Hyperactivity Disorder (ADHD) is a
neurodevelopmental condition characterized by persistent patterns of
inattention, impulsivity, and hyperactivity that extend into adulthood.
While often associated with childhood, ADHD can continue to shape
cognitive processes, behavior, and daily functioning as individuals
transition into adulthood. The core symptoms include difficulty
sustaining attention, impulsive decision-making, and heightened
activity levels.

Dispelling Common Myths:

1. Myth: ADHD is just a lack of focus.
   Reality: ADHD involves a complex interplay of neurobiological factors, affecting not only attention but also impulse control, organization, and executive functions.

2. Myth: ADHD is only a childhood condition.
   - Reality: ADHD frequently persists into adulthood. Its manifestations may evolve, but the impact on daily life, relationships, and work can endure.

3. Myth: Everyone with ADHD is hyperactive.
   - Reality: Hyperactivity is one aspect of ADHD, but not everyone with the condition experiences it. In adults, symptoms may manifest as restlessness or inner turmoil.

4. Myth: ADHD is a result of bad parenting or lack of discipline.
   - Reality: ADHD has a strong genetic component and is linked to neurobiological differences. It is not caused by parenting style or lack of discipline.

5. Myth: ADHD is an excuse for laziness.
   - Reality: Individuals with ADHD often expend more mental energy to accomplish tasks. The challenges they face are rooted in neurological differences, not laziness.

6. Myth: Medication is the only effective treatment for ADHD.
   - Reality: While medication can be a helpful component of treatment, a comprehensive approach may include behavioral therapies, lifestyle adjustments, and support systems.

Understanding Adult ADHD requires dispelling these myths and recognizing the nuanced nature of the condition. By doing so, we pave the way for greater empathy, informed support, and effective strategies to help individuals with ADHD lead fulfilling lives.

the impact of ADHD on daily life, relationships, and work.

Impact of ADHD on Daily Life are as follows:

1. Time Management Challenges: - ADHD can make it difficult to manage time effectively, leading to procrastination, missed deadlines, and a sense of time slipping away.

2. Organization Struggles: - Daily tasks, from keeping a tidy living space to managing personal responsibilities, may become challenging due to difficulties with organization and planning.

3. Inconsistent Focus: - Sustaining attention on routine or mundane tasks may be challenging, resulting in a tendency to bounce between activities.

Impact of ADHD on Relationships:

1. Communication Hurdles: - Difficulty maintaining focus in conversations can lead to misunderstandings, with partners, family, or friends feeling unheard or neglected.

2. Impulsivity in Interactions: - Impulsive behaviors, such as speaking without thinking, can impact relationships, causing tension or misunderstandings.

3. Emotional Regulation: - Managing emotions can be challenging, leading to heightened emotional responses or difficulties in expressing feelings appropriately.

Impact of ADHD on Work:

1. Task Initiation and Completion: - Starting tasks and seeing them through to completion can be a struggle, affecting productivity and work output.

2. Time Management in the Workplace: - Meeting deadlines and managing time effectively at work may pose challenges, impacting job performance.

3. Organizational Skills: - Difficulty organizing work tasks and maintaining a structured work environment can affect efficiency and job satisfaction.

Understanding these impacts is crucial for developing tailored strategies to navigate daily life, nurture relationships, and succeed in the workplace despite the challenges associated with Adult ADHD. It emphasizes the importance of a holistic approach to support and management, encompassing lifestyle adjustments, therapeutic interventions, and a supportive network.

Preventing adult ADHD

Preventing adult ADHD is challenging since it often stems from a combination of genetic, environmental, and neurological factors. However, there are strategies that can help manage symptoms and potentially reduce the impact of ADHD. Here are some preventive measures:

1.   Early Intervention in Childhood:
   Addressing ADHD symptoms in childhood through early intervention, such as behavioral therapy, psychoeducation, and, in some cases, medication, may help mitigate the long-term impact of ADHD.

2.   Educational Support:
   Providing educational support tailored to the individual needs of children with ADHD can contribute to better academic outcomes. This might include accommodations, specialized learning strategies, and targeted interventions.

3.   Parenting Strategies:
   Teaching parents effective parenting strategies, such as consistent discipline, clear communication, and the establishment of routines, can contribute to a more supportive and structured environment for children with ADHD.

4.   Healthy Lifestyle Choices:
   Encouraging a healthy lifestyle, including regular physical activity, balanced nutrition, and adequate sleep, can support overall well-being and potentially help manage ADHD symptoms.

5.   Mindfulness and Coping Skills:

Introducing mindfulness and coping skills early on can help children develop effective ways of managing stress and improving attention and impulse control.

6.   Limiting Environmental Toxins:
While not a direct prevention measure, minimizing exposure to environmental toxins during pregnancy and early childhood may have indirect benefits. This includes avoiding tobacco smoke, alcohol, and certain pollutants.

7.   Identifying and Managing Coexisting Conditions:
Recognizing and addressing coexisting conditions, such as learning disabilities or mental health issues, can be an important aspect of prevention by addressing factors that may exacerbate ADHD symptoms.

8.   Building a Supportive Community:
Creating a supportive community that fosters understanding and acceptance can be crucial for individuals with ADHD. Reducing stigma and providing resources for education and support can contribute to a more inclusive environment.

9.   Research and Awareness:
Continued research into the causes and risk factors of ADHD can lead to improved prevention strategies. Raising awareness about ADHD and its early signs may also contribute to earlier intervention and support.

It's important to note that while these strategies may help manage symptoms and improve outcomes, there is no guaranteed prevention for adult ADHD. Genetic and neurobiological factors play a significant role, and each individual's experience with ADHD is unique. If you suspect ADHD or are concerned about symptoms, it's advisable to consult with healthcare professionals for an accurate diagnosis and appropriate guidance.

Chapter 3:Identify and celebrate the unique strengths associated with ADHD.

In the mosaic of human abilities, the strengths associated with Adult Attention Deficit Hyperactivity Disorder (ADHD) are often overlooked, eclipsed by a focus on challenges. Yet, within the whirlwind of ADHD's characteristics, unique and valuable strengths emerge, waiting to be recognized and celebrated.

1. Creativity Unleashed:ADHD often brings a heightened sense of creativity and innovative thinking. Individuals with ADHD may possess a knack for thinking outside the box, finding unconventional solutions, and approaching challenges with fresh perspectives.

2. Hyperfocus Superpower:While attention may be fleeting in some situations, individuals with ADHD can experience hyperfocus—an intense concentration on a task they find engaging. This hyperfocus can lead to remarkable productivity and mastery in areas of deep interest.

3.Energetic Drive:A surplus of energy is a hallmark of ADHD. When harnessed effectively, this energy becomes a powerful force driving passion and enthusiasm. It can fuel ambitious endeavors and the pursuit of goals with unwavering determination.

4. Adaptability in Dynamic Environments:The ability to thrive in dynamic, fast-paced environments is a strength associated with ADHD. Rapid adaptation to changing circumstances and a comfort with unpredictability can be advantageous in various professional and personal settings.

5. Keen Intuition:Many individuals with ADHD possess a heightened intuition and perceptive awareness of their surroundings. This intuitive insight can lead to quick decision-making and a unique understanding of complex situations.

6. Resilience in the Face of Challenges:Living with ADHD cultivates resilience. The ability to navigate through a world that may not always align with one's cognitive processes fosters a resilient spirit that can weather setbacks and bounce back from adversity.

Recognizing and embracing these strengths is not just an acknowledgment; it is a celebration. It is an affirmation that ADHD is not solely defined by its challenges but enriched by a tapestry of abilities waiting to be explored. By acknowledging these strengths, individuals with ADHD can embark on a journey of self-discovery and empowerment, unlocking their full potential and contributing uniquely to the world around them.

successful individuals who have harnessed their ADHD traits for success.

Success Stories: Embracing ADHD Traits

1. Richard Branson: The charismatic founder of the Virgin Group, Richard Branson, attributes his success in entrepreneurship to his ADHD. His ability to think creatively, take risks, and maintain an unrelenting drive has propelled him to create a diverse and successful business empire.

2. Sir Ken Robinson:Renowned for his work in education and creativity, the late Sir Ken Robinson embraced his ADHD traits to fuel his imaginative thinking. His ability to see beyond conventional

boundaries allowed him to advocate for a more creative and personalized approach to education.

3.Howie Mandel:Comedian, actor, and TV host Howie Mandel has openly discussed his experience with ADHD. His quick wit and improvisational skills, often associated with ADHD, have been instrumental in his successful career in the entertainment industry.

4. Temple Grandin:Dr. Temple Grandin, a world-renowned autism advocate and professor, credits her unique way of thinking, which includes elements of ADHD, for her groundbreaking work in animal science. Her ability to see the world from a different perspective has led to innovations in animal welfare.

5. Michael Phelps:Olympic swimmer Michael Phelps, the most decorated Olympian in history, openly discusses his ADHD diagnosis. His hyperfocus, discipline, and determination have been crucial in his training and competitive success, demonstrating that ADHD traits can be powerful assets.

6. Justin Timberlake:Singer, actor, and entrepreneur Justin Timberlake has spoken about his experience with ADHD. His dynamic performances and multitasking abilities on stage showcase how ADHD traits, when harnessed, can contribute to a thriving career in the entertainment industry.

These individuals exemplify that ADHD traits, when embraced and channeled effectively, can be sources of strength and success. Their stories emphasize that neurodiversity is not a barrier to achievement but a unique lens through which innovation, creativity, and resilience can flourish.

Chapter 4: Building a Support System

To build a Support System as an ADHD Person, you to take the following steps:

1. Open Communication: Share your ADHD diagnosis with close friends, family, and colleagues. Open communication fosters understanding, allowing those around you to offer support and make accommodations when needed.

2. Educate Your Support Network:Provide information about ADHD to help others understand its nuances. This can dispel misconceptions and create a foundation for empathetic support.

3. Set Clear Expectations:Clearly communicate your needs and expectations. Whether it's about time management, organization, or specific accommodations, setting clear expectations helps others support you effectively.

4. Identify Advocates:- Identify individuals within your support network who can serve as advocates. This might include family members, friends, or colleagues who understand ADHD and can help explain it to others if necessary.

5. Professional Support:- Consider seeking professional support from therapists, counselors, or ADHD coaches. These individuals can provide guidance, coping strategies, and a structured approach to managing challenges.

6. Join ADHD Communities:- Connect with others who have ADHD. Online or local support groups provide a platform to share experiences, tips, and encouragement. Being part of a community that understands your journey can be immensely beneficial.

7. Build Routine and Structure:- Work with your support system to establish routines and structures that accommodate your ADHD. Consistency and predictability can contribute to a more supportive environment.

8. Encourage Positive Reinforcement:- Request positive reinforcement from your support network. Acknowledgement and encouragement for your efforts can boost confidence and motivation.

9. Utilize Technology:- Leverage technology to aid in organization and time management. Apps, reminders, and productivity tools can be valuable assets in your daily life.

10. Regular Check-Ins:- Schedule regular check-ins with key members of your support system. This provides an opportunity to discuss challenges, celebrate successes, and adjust strategies as needed.

Building a robust support system involves collaboration, understanding, and a willingness to adapt. By actively engaging with those around you and fostering a supportive environment, you can navigate the challenges of ADHD more effectively and build a foundation for personal and professional success.

The Importance of a Strong Support Network for ADHD Individuals:
1. Emotional Support:
   - A strong support network provides emotional understanding and empathy. It offers a safe space to express frustrations, challenges, and victories, reducing feelings of isolation.

2. Encouragement and Motivation:.
   - Supportive individuals can offer encouragement and motivation,
crucial for maintaining focus, resilience, and a positive mindset in the
face of ADHD-related challenges.

3. Practical Assistance:
   - A support network can provide practical assistance in organizing
tasks, managing time, and addressing daily responsibilities. This
assistance helps mitigate the impact of executive function challenges.

4. Education and Awareness:
   - A support network that is informed about ADHD can contribute to
increased awareness and understanding. This reduces stigma and
fosters an environment where individuals with ADHD feel accepted
and valued.

5. Advocacy:
   - Friends, family, or colleagues who understand ADHD can serve as
advocates, helping to explain the condition to others and facilitating
necessary accommodations in various aspects of life, including work
and social settings.

6. Problem-Solving Together:
   - Collaborative problem-solving becomes more effective with a
strong support network. Discussing challenges and brainstorming
solutions with understanding individuals can lead to innovative
strategies for managing ADHD-related issues.

7. Reducing Isolation:
   - ADHD can sometimes make individuals feel isolated or
misunderstood. A supportive network helps counteract this by
fostering a sense of belonging and connection.

8. Building Confidence:
   - Regular positive interactions within a support network contribute
to building confidence. Feeling valued and supported enhances
self-esteem and empowers individuals with ADHD to face challenges
with greater assurance.

9. Crisis Intervention:
 - During particularly challenging times, a support network can be a
crucial resource for crisis intervention. Whether it's providing a
listening ear or offering practical help, having a reliable network can
make a significant difference.

10. Celebrating Achievements:
   - A strong support network celebrates successes, no matter how
small. Recognizing achievements, milestones, and progress reinforces
a positive outlook and motivates continued effort.

In essence, a robust support network acts as a foundation for
well-being, resilience, and success for individuals with ADHD. It
creates an environment where challenges are faced collectively,
strengths are celebrated, and the journey is navigated with
understanding and compassion.

**tips for communicating your ADHD needs to friends, family,
and colleagues.**

1. Choose the Right Time and Setting:
   - Select a calm and private setting to discuss your ADHD needs.
Avoid rushed or stressful moments for more effective communication.

2. Be Direct and Clear:

-Clearly articulate your needs and challenges associated with ADHD. Use straightforward language to convey your thoughts and feelings.

3. Share Educational Resources:
   - Provide informational resources about ADHD to help others understand the condition better. This can dispel myths and foster a more informed conversation.

4. Express Your Feelings:
   - Share how ADHD affects you emotionally and cognitively. This personal touch helps others connect with your experience on a deeper level.

5. Use "I" Statements:
   - Frame your communication using "I" statements to express your thoughts and feelings without sounding accusatory. For example, say, "I sometimes struggle with time management" instead of "You never understand my schedule."

6. Highlight Strengths:
   - Emphasize the strengths associated with ADHD. Help your friends, family, or colleagues understand that ADHD is not just about challenges but also unique abilities.

7. Provide Specific Ex
   - Illustrate your challenges and needs with concrete examples. This makes it easier for others to comprehend and visualize how ADHD manifests in your daily life.

8. Set Clear Expectations:
   - Clearly define your expectations regarding support or accommodations. Whether it's regarding communication styles,

deadlines, or organizational strategies, be specific about what would be helpful.

9. Encourage Questions:
   - Create an open dialogue by encouraging questions. This allows others to seek clarification and demonstrates your willingness to engage in a collaborative conversation.

10. Discuss Coping Strategies:
   - Share coping strategies that work for you and discuss how others can support these efforts. This collaborative approach involves them in finding practical solutions.

11. Highlight External Triggers:
   - Identify external factors or triggers that may exacerbate ADHD symptoms. Discuss how these factors can be mitigated to create a more supportive environment.

12. Revisit the Conversation Periodically:
   - ADHD needs can evolve over time. Schedule periodic check-ins to discuss how things are going, what adjustments may be needed, and to ensure ongoing understanding.

Effective communication about ADHD needs is a crucial step in fostering understanding and creating a supportive environment. By approaching these conversations with transparency, empathy, and a collaborative spirit, you can build stronger connections with friends, family, and colleagues.

Chapter 5: Time Management and Organization

Practical Techniques for Managing Time Effectively with ADHD:

1. Use Visual Timers: - Set visual timers or alarms to help manage time intervals for tasks. This provides a clear visual cue and helps maintain focus on specific activities.

2. Break Tasks Into Smaller Steps:- Divide larger tasks into smaller, more manageable steps. This makes it easier to approach and complete tasks without feeling overwhelmed.

3. Prioritize Tasks:- Prioritize tasks based on importance and deadlines. Focus on high-priority items first to ensure critical responsibilities are addressed promptly.

4. Time Blocking:
   - Allocate specific blocks of time to different tasks or activities. This structured approach helps create a routine and provides a visual representation of how time is spent.

5. Set Realistic Goals:
   - Establish realistic and achievable goals for each day. Avoid overloading your schedule, as this can lead to stress and reduced productivity.

6. Use a Planner or Digital Calendar:

- Utilize planners or digital calendars to organize and schedule tasks.
Set reminders for deadlines and appointments to help stay on track.

7. Create To-Do Lists:
   - Break down daily tasks into a to-do list. Check off items as you
complete them, providing a sense of accomplishment and helping you
stay focused.

8. Limit Distractions:
   - Identify and minimize potential distractions. Create a dedicated
workspace, turn off non-essential notifications, and consider using
noise-canceling headphones if needed.

9. Practice Mindfulness:
   - Incorporate mindfulness techniques to stay present and focused.
Techniques such as deep breathing or brief meditation can help center
your attention.

10. Use External Reminders:
   - Place visual cues or reminders in your environment. Sticky notes,
alarms, or color-coded reminders can serve as prompts for specific
tasks.

11. Chunk Similar Tasks Together:
   - Group similar tasks together during specific time blocks. This
minimizes mental transitions and enhances efficiency.

12. Reward Yourself:
   - Implement a reward system to reinforce positive behavior.
Celebrate completing tasks with a small break, a favorite snack, or
another enjoyable activity.

13. Delegate When Possible:

- Delegate tasks when appropriate. This helps distribute the workload and ensures tasks are completed efficiently.

14. Stay Flexible:
   - Recognize that plans may need adjustment. Be flexible and adaptable, allowing for changes without causing undue stress.

15. Review and Reflect:
   - Regularly review your schedule and reflect on what works best for you. Adjust your time management strategies based on your evolving understanding of your strengths and challenges.

Experiment with these techniques to find a combination that works best for you. Consistency and adaptability are key as you develop effective time management strategies tailored to your unique strengths and needs.

Organizational Strategies Tailored to the ADHD Mindset:

1. Visual Organization:
   - Use visual tools like color-coded folders, sticky notes, or visual charts to organize information. Visual cues can enhance memory and make it easier to locate items.

2. Create a Dedicated Workspace:
   - Establish a clutter-free and organized workspace. Having a designated area for tasks can help minimize distractions and create a structured environment.

3. Use Technology Wisely:

- Leverage productivity apps and tools designed to help with organization. Digital calendars, task management apps, and reminders can assist in keeping track of appointments and deadlines.

4. Daily Checklists:
  - Create daily checklists for tasks. Breaking down responsibilities into manageable steps and checking them off provides a sense of accomplishment.

5. Time-Blocking for Tasks:
  - Allocate specific time blocks for different tasks throughout the day. This helps in managing time effectively and maintaining focus on one task at a time.

6. Implement Routines:
  - Establish consistent routines for daily activities. Predictability and structure can be beneficial for individuals with ADHD.

7. Use Memory Aids:
  - Employ memory aids such as mnemonic devices, acronyms, or visual cues to enhance recall. These aids can be particularly helpful for remembering details.

8. Limit Options:
  - Simplify choices by limiting options. For instance, organize your wardrobe with fewer choices to make getting ready in the morning more straightforward.

9. Delegate and Outsource:
  - Delegate tasks when possible, and outsource activities that may be particularly challenging. This can help distribute the workload and reduce overwhelm.

10. Organize in Batches:
   - Group similar tasks together and tackle them in batches. This
minimizes the need for constant switching between different types of
activities.

11. Use Memory Hooks:
   - Associate information with memorable cues or hooks. Making
connections between new information and existing knowledge aids in
retention.

12. Regular Decluttering:
   - Schedule regular decluttering sessions to keep your physical and
digital spaces organized. This prevents the buildup of chaos and makes
it easier to find what you need.

13. Utilize Reminders and Alarms:
   - Set reminders and alarms for important tasks or deadlines. This
ensures that you stay on track and reduces the likelihood of forgetting
essential commitments.

14. Mind Mapping:
   - Use mind maps to visually represent information and relationships
between ideas. This technique can be a creative and effective way to
organize thoughts and concepts.

15. Celebrate Small Wins:
   - Acknowledge and celebrate small organizational victories.
Recognizing achievements, no matter how minor, can provide
motivation to maintain organizational efforts.

Tailoring organizational strategies to the ADHD mindset involves
embracing creativity, flexibility, and personalized approaches.

Experiment with different techniques to discover what works best for your individual needs and preferences.

Chapter 6: Enhancing Focus and Productivity

Mindfulness and Meditation Techniques for Improving Focus with ADHD,To enhance your focus you to do the following :

1. Mindful Breathing:
   - Practice mindful breathing exercises. Focus on your breath, inhaling and exhaling slowly. When your mind wanders, gently bring your attention back to your breath.

2. Body Scan Meditation:
   - Engage in a body scan meditation, where you systematically focus your attention on different parts of your body. This helps cultivate awareness and reduce overall stress.

3. Guided Meditation:
   - Use guided meditation sessions specifically designed for ADHD. Apps or online platforms often offer guided sessions that cater to the unique challenges of maintaining focus.

4. Walking Meditation:
   - Combine mindfulness with physical activity through walking meditation. Pay attention to each step, your breath, and the sensations in your body as you walk.

5. Mindful Eating:
   - Practice mindful eating by savoring each bite, paying attention to textures, flavors, and smells. This can enhance present-moment awareness and focus.

6. Visualization Techniques:
   - Utilize visualization exercises to create a mental image that promotes calm and focus. Picture a serene place or a specific goal, engaging your senses in the visualization.

7. Focused Attention Meditation:
   - Choose a specific focal point, such as your breath, a sound, or an object. Concentrate your attention on this point and gently guide your mind back if distractions arise.

8. Mindful Listening:
   - Practice mindful listening by fully engaging in the sounds around you. Focus on individual sounds, their intensity, and their duration to enhance your present awareness.

9. Mindfulness Apps:
   - Explore mindfulness apps that offer structured programs for ADHD. These apps often incorporate guided meditations, progress tracking, and reminders for regular practice.

10. Yoga for Mindfulness:
   - Engage in yoga practices that emphasize mindfulness. Combining gentle movements with breath awareness can promote focus and relaxation.

11. Mindful Journaling:
   - Journaling with a focus on the present moment can be a mindfulness practice. Describe your thoughts and feelings, and explore the sensations you experience.

12. Loving-Kindness Meditation:

- Practice loving-kindness meditation by directing positive and compassionate thoughts toward yourself and others. This can enhance emotional well-being and focus.

13. Set Intention for the Day:
   - Begin your day by setting a mindful intention. This can help create a positive mindset and guide your focus throughout the day.

14. Progressive Muscle Relaxation:
   - Combine mindfulness with relaxation through progressive muscle relaxation. Gradually tense and then release different muscle groups, paying attention to the sensations.

15. Mindfulness in Daily Activities:
   - Integrate mindfulness into daily activities, such as washing dishes or walking. Pay full attention to the sensory experience of each activity, fostering a state of focused awareness.

Consistent practice of these mindfulness and meditation techniques can contribute to improved focus, attention, and overall well-being for individuals with ADHD. Experiment with different approaches to find what resonates best with you.

Productivity Hacks for Individuals with ADHD:

   1. Pomodoro Technique:
   - Break tasks into short, focused intervals (e.g., 25 minutes), followed by a brief break. This helps maintain attention and prevents burnout.

   2. ask Batching:
   - Group similar tasks together during specific time blocks. This minimizes context-switching and enhances overall efficiency.

3. Use Visual Cues:
   - Create visual reminders and cues to prompt action.
Color-coded sticky notes, alarms, or visual timers can help keep
you on track.

4. Time Blocking:
   - Allocate specific blocks of time for different activities. This
creates a structured schedule and reduces the overwhelming
feeling of having too much to do.

5. Externalize Memory:
   - Use external tools like calendars, task lists, and reminders to
offload memory demands. This reduces the risk of forgetting
important tasks.

6. Mind Maps for Planning:
   - Utilize mind maps to visually organize thoughts and tasks.
This technique provides a clear overview and helps in planning.

7. Digital Task Management Apps:
   - Leverage productivity apps with features like reminders, due
dates, and task categorization. These apps can provide structure
and organization.

8. Set Clear Goals:
   - Define clear and specific goals for each task. Knowing what
needs to be achieved increases motivation and helps maintain
focus.

9. Limit Open Tabs and Apps:

- Minimize digital distractions by limiting the number of open tabs or apps. Focus on one task at a time to avoid information overload.

10. Structured To-Do Lists:
   - Create structured to-do lists with priorities. Break down tasks into smaller steps and check them off as you complete them for a sense of accomplishment.

11. Use Positive Reinforcement:
   - Implement a reward system for completing tasks. Positive reinforcement can be a powerful motivator for individuals with ADHD.

12. Delegate Non-Essential Tasks:
   - Delegate tasks that others can handle. This allows you to focus on high-priority activities and reduces overall workload.

13. Utilize Hyperfocus Moments:
   - Identify and harness hyperfocus moments when concentration is naturally heightened. Channel this intense focus into tasks that require sustained attention.

14. Create a Dedicated Workspace:
   - Designate a specific workspace for tasks. Having a dedicated environment signals to your brain that it's time to focus.

15. Mindful Transitions:
   - Incorporate short mindfulness exercises during transitions between tasks. This helps reset your focus and promotes a calm and centered mindset.

16. Automate Routine Tasks:

- Automate repetitive and routine tasks whenever possible. This streamlines processes and reduces the mental load.

17.Break Down Large Tasks:
   - Divide larger tasks into smaller, more manageable steps. Tackling these smaller components makes the overall task less daunting.

18. External Accountability:
   - Share your goals with a friend or family member who can provide external accountability. Regular check-ins can help you stay on track.

Experiment with these productivity hacks and tailor them to your preferences. Finding a combination that works for your individual needs can significantly enhance your ability to stay focused and productive.
Eliminating distractions for adults with ADHD involves implementing strategies that promote focus and minimize external disruptions. Here are some tips to help manage distractions:

1. Create a Dedicated Workspace:
   Establish a dedicated and organized workspace that is free from unnecessary distractions. Minimize clutter and create an environment conducive to concentration.

2. Use Tools and Technology:
   Leverage tools and apps designed to increase productivity. There are various apps that can help block distracting websites or provide reminders for tasks.

3. Break Tasks Into Smaller Steps:

Divide larger tasks into smaller, more manageable steps. This
can make it easier to stay focused and reduce the feeling of being
overwhelmed.

4. Prioritize Tasks:
Prioritize tasks based on importance and deadlines. Focusing
on high-priority tasks first can help prevent procrastination.

5. Set Clear Goals:
Clearly define your goals for each task. Knowing what you need
to accomplish provides a sense of direction and purpose,
reducing the likelihood of distractions.

6. Establish a Routine:
Set and stick to a daily routine. Consistency can help train your
brain to focus during specific periods and reduce distractions.

7. Time Blocking:
Use time-blocking techniques to allocate specific periods for
different tasks. During these dedicated times, focus solely on the
task at hand and avoid distractions.

8. Limit Multitasking:
While multitasking might seem efficient, it can often lead to
increased distractions. Focus on one task at a time to improve
overall productivity.

9. Implement Breaks:
Schedule short breaks between tasks to refresh your mind. This
can prevent mental fatigue and help maintain focus when
returning to work.

10. Use Noise-Canceling Headphones:

If ambient noise is distracting, consider using noise-canceling headphones. They can help create a quieter environment and improve concentration.

11. Practice Mindfulness and Meditation:
Incorporate mindfulness techniques and meditation into your routine. These practices can enhance your ability to stay present and focused.

12. Seek Support and Accountability:
Share your goals with a friend, family member, or colleague who can provide support and hold you accountable. Having someone to check in with can help maintain focus.

13. Set Realistic Expectations:
Be realistic about what you can achieve within a given timeframe. Avoid setting overly ambitious goals that may lead to frustration and distraction.

14. Consider Professional Support:
Consult with mental health professionals, such as therapists or coaches specializing in ADHD. They can provide tailored strategies and support for managing distractions.

Remember that finding the right combination of strategies may require some experimentation. It's essential to be patient with yourself and to make adjustments as needed to create a personalized plan for minimizing distractions.

Chapter 7: Overcoming Challenges at Work

Workplace Strategies to Navigate Challenges and Leverage ADHD Strengths:

1. Open Communication:
  - Communicate openly with supervisors and colleagues about your ADHD. Discuss your strengths and challenges to foster understanding and create a supportive work environment.

2. Identify Optimal Work Conditions:
  - Determine the conditions that help you focus best. Whether it's a quiet workspace, specific lighting, or certain tools, advocate for an environment that enhances your productivity.

3. Use Time Management Tools:
  - Utilize time management tools such as calendars, reminders, and task lists to help organize and prioritize work tasks. This helps prevent feeling overwhelmed by deadlines.

4. Set Clear Goals and Deadlines:
  - Clearly define goals and deadlines for tasks. Breaking down projects into smaller, manageable goals makes the workload more digestible.

5. Leverage Hyperfocus:
  - Identify tasks that align with your interests and strengths, allowing you to tap into hyperfocus moments. Use these periods of intense concentration to accomplish significant tasks.

6. Implement Structured Breaks:

- Schedule short, structured breaks to prevent burnout and maintain focus. This could involve quick walks, deep breathing exercises, or mindfulness practices.

7. Seek Varied Tasks:
  - Advocate for a variety of tasks in your role. Having a mix of responsibilities can help prevent monotony and keep your attention engaged.

8. Provide Clear Instructions:
  - Request clear and explicit instructions for tasks. Clarity in expectations can help you navigate assignments more effectively.

9. Utilize Assistive Technologies:
  - Explore assistive technologies that can aid in organization and time management. Apps, tools, and software designed for ADHD can be valuable assets.

10. Regular Check-Ins:
  - Schedule regular check-ins with supervisors or team members to discuss progress, challenges, and adjustments. This ongoing communication ensures everyone is on the same page.

11. Delegate Appropriately:
  - Identify tasks that can be delegated to colleagues based on their strengths. Delegating appropriately allows you to focus on tasks that align with your skills.

12. Continuous Learning and Skill Development:
  - Embrace opportunities for continuous learning and skill development. Engaging in activities that stimulate your interests can enhance motivation and focus.

13. Create a Structured Routine:
   - Establish a structured routine for your workday. Consistency in daily activities helps create a predictable and manageable work environment.

14. Use Positive Reinforcement:
   - Implement a system of positive reinforcement for meeting goals and deadlines. Celebrate achievements, fostering a positive work atmosphere.

15. Advocate for Flexibility:
   - Discuss and negotiate flexible work arrangements when possible. Flexibility in work hours or remote work can provide an environment that suits your individual needs.

By proactively implementing these workplace strategies, individuals with ADHD can navigate challenges effectively and capitalize on their unique strengths, contributing positively to the work environment. Buy in

How grown-ups can oversee ADHD without a prescription

There are techniques grown-ups can use to oversee consideration shortfall hyperactivity jumble (ADHD) without prescription. For instance, learning new efficiency methodologies might help.

Ordinary activity, adjusted nourishment, and techniques to help rest may likewise assist with decreasing side effects. An individual can give these methodologies a shot on their own, or with the assistance of an accomplished mentor or specialist.

Be that as it may, it is vital to perceive when an individual necessities extra assistance as clinical treatment.

Peruse on to dive deeper into the techniques that can assist with overseeing ADHD without medicine for grown-ups.

Practice and outside time

The research proposes that standard activity assists with decreasing the side effects of ADHD, both temporarily and over the long run.

A 2017 orderly survey found that both cardio and different types of activity could have benefits, however, cardio showed specific advantages for:

working on leader capability, which is the capacity to intellectually design out errands and control conduct

further developing consideration

decreasing impulsivity

A few grown-ups with ADHD likewise report that being outside and in touch with nature helps their side effects. There isn't a lot of examination of the effect of this methodology on grown-ups.

Nonetheless, a more seasoned study trusted by Wellspring of Kids found that outside after-school exercises appeared to diminish side effects more than indoor exercises. This was valid for kids from a scope of foundations and areas in the US.

The creators propose getting more "green time" every day. If conceivable, a grown-up could do this by:

taking a greener course to work

enjoying reprieves outside, like in a recreation area

tackling errands close to a window with a green view

practicing outside

Rest and ADHD

Many individuals with ADHD experience difficulty resting and waking at customary times. Sunshine openness, particularly toward the beginning of the day, may assist with managing rest plans. Different tips that might help include:

staying away from caffeine at night

utilizing blue light channels on screens

halting the utilization of screens and gadgets past a specific time

following a quieting sleep schedule

reliably heading to sleep and awakening simultaneously

utilizing foundation sound, like background noise, makes a difference

Efficiency Techniques for ADHD

Overseeing undertakings, like everyday tasks, work, studies, or youngster caring liabilities can be difficult for anybody, however, especially for grown-ups with ADHD.

Nonetheless, many individuals with ADHD report that the customary efficiency tips that neurotypical individuals use are not useful for them. Consequently, it might assist with gaining the executive's methodologies from other people who have ADHD.

Episodically, individuals with ADHD report that it serves to:

Begin little: Attempting to do the hardest errands initially can be overpowering to individuals with ADHD and may bring about delay. All things considered, begin with one little errand, like washing one dish or perusing one page of a book. This can assist with igniting further inspiration by giving somebody a little success.

Use clocks: Certain individuals with ADHD find that having a cutoff time assists them with centering. Utilizing a clock can make a similar impact and give an individual a substantial time when the errand will wrap up. For instance, an individual could set a clock for an hour to clean their home.

Body twofold: This implies having someone else sit in the room while somebody does an undertaking. They could be doing a similar assignment or something different. They can be close by to assist with deterrents.

For recalling errands, it might likewise serve to:

Set up programmed updates: Pick a booking or schedule application, and set up programmed updates for significant errands. This could incorporate any repetitive errands or occasions, like tasks, arrangements, or birthday celebrations.

Utilize noticeable updates: It might assist with having a schedule on the wall, or a dry-delete board, where an individual can compose significant wake-up calls.

Rearrange the home: Changing where items are in the home might assist an individual with recollecting where they are and noticing when they need to tackle undertakings. For instance, involving clear holders for food permits individuals to effortlessly track down things in cabinets and see when they need to restock.

If an individual finds it overwhelming to roll out these improvements all alone, enrolling the assistance of a companion, accomplice, or relative might help.

Another choice is working with an ADHD mentor. These experts can offer help and counsel on the functional parts of ADHD and may assist an individual with arriving at their objectives.

Sustenance for ADHD

A 2022 precise survey expresses that there is restricted proof that diet can assist grown-ups with ADHD. Many elements can impact ADHD side effects, which makes testing the effect of diet alone challenging to do.

Notwithstanding, a few past examinations have found that a few healthfully adjusted ones consume fewer calories, for example, the Mediterranean and Run eat less, have connections to diminished ADHD side effects in youngsters.

There is additionally some proof that individuals with ADHD might be more inclined to nutrient and mineral insufficiencies. For instance, a more seasoned 2016 investigation discovered that individuals with ADHD conclusion were bound to lack in:

vitamin B2

vitamin B6

nutrient B9

It is hazy if this assumes a part in the improvement of ADHD, or whether it is the consequence of unpredictable eating designs. Nonetheless, the analysts noticed that side effects would in general be more serious in individuals with vitamin B2 and B6 insufficiencies, which recommends that tending to any supplement could help.

As indicated by a 2018 survey, there is likewise some proof that polyunsaturated unsaturated fats, like Omega-3, may affect ADHD side effects.

Psychotherapy for ADHD

Psychotherapy, or talk treatment, isn't a remedy for ADHD. However, it might assist an individual with mastering adapting abilities, and direct feelings, or address the effect of pessimistic informing and disgrace around the condition.

Conducting treatment is one choice. This spotlights assisting an individual with overseeing ways of behaving that are obstructing their life.

Treatment can likewise assist with low confidence and relationship troubles, and the sky's the limit from there. Individuals might find it valuable to search for a specialist with experience assisting those with ADHD and who grasps neurodiversity.

For peer support, there are numerous on the web and in-person help gatherings, where grown-ups with ADHD can find individuals who share comparative encounters.

Outline

There are numerous ways of overseeing ADHD without drugs, including making sound rest propensities, tending to nourish lacks, getting standard activity, and learning better approaches for taking care of errands.

What helps every individual might differ, so individuals might find it valuable to attempt each new methodology in turn. This can provide them with a thought of what works for them.

Be that as it may, anybody experiencing issues with their side effects, or with their emotional well-being, ought to address a clinical expert about treatment choices

Advice for Disclosing ADHD in a Professional Setting:

1. Assess Your Workplace Culture:
   - Gauge the workplace culture and policies regarding neurodiversity and disabilities. Understanding the environment can inform your decision on whether and how to disclose.

2. Timing Matters:
   - Choose an appropriate time to disclose, ideally when you have established a level of trust and familiarity with your supervisor or HR. Consider discussing it during a one-on-one meeting.

3. Focus on Accommodations:
   - Emphasize the accommodations you may need to perform at your best rather than just disclosing the diagnosis. Highlighting specific needs shows your commitment to productivity.

4. Prepare Information:
- Equip yourself with information about ADHD, its impact, and common accommodations. This can help in educating others and dispelling misconceptions.

5. Be Positive and Solution-Oriented:
   - Frame the conversation positively, emphasizing your strengths and the unique perspective you bring to the workplace. Discuss potential solutions and how you've successfully managed challenges in the past.

6. Use "I" Statements:
   - Share your experience using "I" statements to make it a personal, individual conversation. This helps others understand your perspective without feeling blamed.

7. Highlight Past Successes:
   - Share examples of your past successes and contributions to the organization. This underscores your capability and demonstrates that ADHD does not define your potential.

8. Consider Privacy Preferences:
   - Determine the level of detail you're comfortable disclosing. You might choose to share only with your immediate supervisor or with HR, depending on your privacy preferences.

9. Educate, Don't Assume Knowledge:

- Recognize that not everyone may be familiar with ADHD. Be prepared to provide basic information and correct any misconceptions that may arise.

10. Request a Follow-Up Meeting:
   - If necessary, request a follow-up meeting to discuss potential accommodations or any further questions your supervisor may have. This allows for continued open communication.

11. Know Your Rights:
   - Familiarize yourself with workplace rights related to disabilities. Understanding your rights can empower you during discussions about accommodations.

12. Connect with Employee Assistance Programs:
   - Explore if your workplace has Employee Assistance Programs (EAPs) that can provide support and resources for employees facing personal or professional challenges.

13. Be Confident:
   - Approach the conversation with confidence. Confidence in your abilities and the value you bring to the workplace can positively influence perceptions.

14. Consider Writing:
   - If verbal communication is challenging, consider putting your thoughts in writing. This allows you to carefully articulate your message and provides a reference for future discussions.

15. Seek Professional Advice:
   - If unsure, seek advice from professionals who specialize in workplace accommodations or disability disclosure. They can offer guidance tailored to your specific situation.

Remember that disclosing ADHD is a personal decision, and you should prioritize your well-being and comfort. The goal is to create an environment that allows you to perform at your best and ensures that your workplace supports your needs.

Chapter 8: Nurturing Relationships

Everyone deserves good Relationship and deserve to be loved and cared for but there are still challenges in nurturing good Relationship, they're:
1. Communication Challenges:
   - ADHD can contribute to communication difficulties, including trouble focusing during conversations, impulsivity in responses, and a tendency to interrupt.

2. Forgetfulness and Distraction:
   - Forgetfulness and distractibility may lead to missed appointments, neglecting responsibilities, and unintentionally overlooking the needs or requests of a partner.

3. Time Management Struggles:
   - Difficulty with time management may result in tardiness or missed deadlines, causing frustration for both partners.

4. Impulsivity in Actions and Words:
   - Impulsivity, a common trait in ADHD, can manifest in impulsive actions or words, potentially leading to misunderstandings or conflicts in relationships.

5. Emotional Dysregulation:
   - Emotional dysregulation, such as mood swings or intense emotional reactions, can impact the emotional climate of the relationship.

6. Task Initiation and Completion:
 - Challenges with initiating and completing tasks may affect shared responsibilities, leading to uneven distribution of household or relationship duties.

7. Inconsistent Focus on Relationships:
 - ADHD individuals may struggle with maintaining consistent focus on their partner or the relationship, creating feelings of neglect.

8. Hyperfocus on Interests:
 - While ADHD can lead to difficulty focusing, it can also result in hyperfocus on specific interests or activities, potentially leading to neglect of other aspects of the relationship.

9. Managing Finances:
 - Impulsivity and challenges with organization may impact financial management, causing stress in the relationship.

10. Frequent Shifts in Interests:
 - ADHD individuals may experience frequent shifts in interests, which can impact shared activities and long-term plans within the relationship.

11. Feeling Overwhelmed:
 - Individuals with ADHD may feel overwhelmed by the demands of daily life, affecting their ability to actively engage in and contribute to the relationship.

12. Coping Strategies and Self-Esteem:
 - Developing effective coping strategies and maintaining self-esteem can be challenging, influencing overall relationship dynamics.

It's important to note that while ADHD can pose challenges in relationships, it doesn't define the potential for success. Understanding and open communication between partners, as well as the implementation of coping strategies and support, can contribute to healthier and more resilient relationships. Seeking professional guidance, such as couples therapy or counseling, can also be beneficial in navigating challenges and enhancing relationship dynamics.

Communication Tips for Maintaining Healthy Connections:

1. Active Listening:
   - Practice active listening by fully focusing on what the other person is saying. This involves making eye contact, nodding, and providing verbal affirmations to show engagement.

2. Empathetic Responses:
   - Respond with empathy, showing that you understand and validate the other person's feelings. This helps build emotional connection and trust.

3. Open and Honest Communication:
   - Foster an environment of open and honest communication. Encourage sharing thoughts and feelings without fear of judgment.

4. Use "I" Statements:
   - Frame your thoughts using "I" statements to express your feelings and perspectives without sounding accusatory. For example, say "I feel..." instead of "You always..."

5. Avoid Blame and Criticism:
   - Refrain from placing blame or criticizing. Instead, focus on expressing your needs and working collaboratively to find solutions.

6. Clarify and Summarize:
   - Clarify information by summarizing what you've heard. This ensures that both parties have a shared understanding of the conversation.

7. Set Boundaries:
   - Establish clear boundaries and communicate them openly. Respect each other's personal space and individual needs.

8. Express Gratitude:
   - Express gratitude for positive actions or qualities in the other person. Acknowledging and appreciating each other strengthens the bond.

9. Mindful Communication:
   - Practice mindful communication by being fully present in the moment. Minimize distractions and give your full attention during conversations.

10. Use Non-Verbal Cues:
   - Pay attention to non-verbal cues such as body language and facial expressions. These can convey emotions that may not be explicitly stated.

11. Regular Check-Ins:
   - Schedule regular check-ins to discuss feelings, concerns, and the overall state of the relationship. This helps prevent misunderstandings from escalating.

12. Seek Understanding:

- Seek to understand the other person's perspective before offering your own. This promotes empathy and demonstrates a willingness to listen.

13. Be Mindful of Tone:
   - Pay attention to the tone of your voice. A respectful and calm tone contributes to a positive communication atmosphere.

14. Use Humor:
   - Incorporate humor when appropriate. Light-hearted moments can ease tension and create a positive communication environment.

15. Apologize and Forgive:
   - Be willing to apologize when necessary and forgive. Resolving conflicts involves acknowledging mistakes and moving forward together.

16. Celebrate Achievements:
   - Celebrate each other's achievements, both big and small. Positive reinforcement strengthens the bond and fosters a supportive atmosphere.

17. Take Breaks During Conflicts:
   - If conflicts arise, take breaks when needed. This allows both parties to cool off and approach the discussion with a clearer mindset.

18. Express Love and Affection:
   - Regularly express love and affection. Verbal affirmations and physical gestures contribute to a nurturing and loving connection.

Effective communication is foundational to healthy relationships. By incorporating these tips, individuals can foster strong connections, promote understanding, and navigate challenges more successfully.

Memory Techniques to Improve Task and Item Recall:

1. Use Checklists:
  - Create checklists for daily tasks and activities. Checking items off a list provides a visual cue of completion and helps prevent forgetting essential tasks.

2. Establish Routines:
  - Develop consistent daily routines. Habits and routines can enhance memory by providing a structured framework for daily activities.

3. Create Associations:
  - Associate new information with familiar concepts or use mnemonic devices. Creating connections can make it easier to recall details later.

4. Visualize Information:
  - Visualize concepts or items you want to remember. Creating mental images can enhance memory retention.

5. Chunk Information:
  - Break down complex information into smaller, manageable chunks. This can make it easier to remember and process.

6. Use Memory Palaces:
  - Create mental images of familiar locations, like your home, and associate specific items or tasks with different rooms. Mentally "place" items in these locations for easier recall.

7. Utilize Acronyms and Initials:
  - Create acronyms or use the first letters of words to remember a sequence or list. This technique is helpful for remembering specific orders or names.

8. Repeat Information Aloud:
  - Saying information aloud can reinforce memory through auditory cues. Repeat key details or tasks to yourself.

9. Write It Down:
  - Use notebooks, planners, or digital apps to jot down important information, tasks, or ideas. Writing reinforces memory and provides a reference for later.

10. Stay Organized:
  - Keep your living and working spaces organized. Knowing where items are located reduces the likelihood of misplacing things.

11. Set Reminders:
  - Use alarms, reminders on your phone, or calendar notifications to prompt you about upcoming tasks or events.

12. Utilize Color Coding:
  - Assign specific colors to different categories or tasks. This visual cue can make it easier to remember and prioritize information.

13. Practice Mindfulness:
  - Engage in mindfulness techniques to stay present and focused on the task at hand. This can enhance overall awareness and memory.

14. Break Tasks Into Steps:
  - Break down large tasks into smaller, more manageable steps. This approach makes it easier to remember and execute each component.

15. Use Memory Apps:
  - Explore memory-enhancing apps designed to help with task management and organization. Some apps provide reminders and prompts to keep you on track.

16. Connect Emotions to Memories:
   - Emotions can strengthen memory. Connect tasks or information to emotions, making it more likely that you'll remember them.

17. Review and Reflect:
   - Regularly review your tasks and priorities. Reflecting on what needs to be done reinforces the information in your memory.

18. Get Adequate Sleep:
   - Ensure you're getting sufficient sleep. Sleep is essential for memory consolidation and overall cognitive function.

Experiment with these memory techniques to find what works best for you. Combining multiple strategies and making them a part of your daily routine can significantly improve your ability to recall tasks, ideas, and the location of items like keys.

Chapter 9: Self-Care for Mental Wellbeing

No matter what You're going through, you need to take care of yourself
. Do the following for your well being:
1. Stress Reduction:
  - Self-care activities, such as relaxation techniques, can help reduce
stress levels. Stress management is crucial for individuals with ADHD,
as stress can exacerbate symptoms.

2. Emotional Regulation:
  - Engaging in self-care practices promotes emotional regulation. This
is particularly beneficial for individuals with ADHD, who may
experience heightened emotional responses.

3. Improved Focus and Attention:
  - Proper self-care, including adequate sleep and nutrition, positively
impacts cognitive function. This can contribute to improved focus and
attention, addressing key challenges associated with ADHD.

4. Enhanced Resilience:
  - Regular self-care builds emotional resilience, helping individuals
better cope with the ups and downs of daily life. This resilience is
valuable for managing the unique challenges that ADHD may present.

5. Prevention of Burnout:
  - Consistent self-care prevents burnout, a common risk for
individuals with ADHD who may experience difficulty managing
energy levels and maintaining focus over extended periods.

6. Better Sleep Patterns:

- Establishing healthy sleep patterns through self-care contributes to overall well-being. Quality sleep is crucial for managing ADHD symptoms and maintaining optimal cognitive function.

7. Balanced Lifestyle:
   - Self-care promotes a balanced lifestyle, encompassing physical, emotional, and social well-being. Balance is key for individuals with ADHD, as extreme fluctuations can impact symptom severity.

8. Enhanced Self-Esteem:
   - Practicing self-care fosters a positive relationship with oneself. This enhanced self-esteem is important for individuals with ADHD, who may face challenges that impact self-perception.

9. Effective Coping Mechanisms:
   - Engaging in self-care activities provides effective coping mechanisms for managing stressors and challenges. This equips individuals with ADHD to navigate daily life more successfully.

10. Positive Impact on Relationships:
   - When individuals prioritize their mental health through self-care, it positively influences relationships. Healthy individuals are better equipped to engage positively in social connections.

11. Mindfulness and Present-Moment Awareness:
   - Self-care often involves mindfulness practices, fostering present-moment awareness. This is particularly beneficial for ADHD individuals, helping them stay focused and grounded.

12. Personalized Coping Strategies:
   - Self-care is highly individualized, allowing individuals with ADHD to discover and implement coping strategies that work best for their unique needs and preferences.

13. Prevention of Overwhelm:
   - Regular self-care prevents the accumulation of stress and overwhelm. Breaking down tasks, taking breaks, and engaging in enjoyable activities contribute to a more manageable daily life.

14. Encourages Healthy Habits:
   - Self-care encourages the development of healthy habits, such as regular exercise, balanced nutrition, and consistent sleep patterns, all of which contribute to improved mental health.

15. Empowerment and Control:
   - Engaging in self-care activities empowers individuals with ADHD to take control of their well-being. This sense of agency is important for managing the various aspects of life impacted by ADHD.

In conclusion, prioritizing self-care is paramount for individuals with ADHD, as it directly contributes to better mental health, improved symptom management, and an overall enhanced quality of life.

Relaxation Techniques and Stress Management Strategies for ADHD:

1. Deep Breathing:
   - Practice deep breathing exercises to calm the nervous system. Inhale deeply through the nose, hold for a few seconds, and exhale slowly through the mouth.

2. Mindfulness Meditation:
   - Engage in mindfulness meditation to cultivate present-moment awareness. Focus on your breath or a specific point of attention to promote relaxation.

3. Progressive Muscle Relaxation (PMR):
   - Progressively tense and then relax different muscle groups throughout the body. This helps release physical tension and induces a state of relaxation.

4. Guided Imagery:
   - Listen to guided imagery recordings or create your own mental images of peaceful and calming scenes. Visualization can help shift focus away from stressors.

5. Yoga and Tai Chi:
   - Participate in yoga or Tai Chi, both of which combine gentle movements with focused breathing. These practices promote relaxation and improve overall well-being.

6. Aromatherapy:
   - Use calming scents like lavender or chamomile through essential oils, candles, or diffusers. Aromatherapy can have a soothing effect on the mind.

7. Journaling:
   - Write down your thoughts and feelings in a journal. Expressing yourself on paper can be a therapeutic way to process emotions and reduce stress.

8. Listening to Music:
   - Create a playlist of calming music and listen to it when feeling stressed. Music can have a profound impact on mood and relaxation.

9. Grounding Techniques:
   - Ground yourself in the present moment by focusing on your senses. Describe the details of your surroundings to yourself, engaging sight, sound, touch, taste, and smell.

10. Break Tasks Into Smaller Steps:
   - When facing a large task, break it into smaller, more manageable steps. This prevents feelings of overwhelm and makes the task more approachable.

11. Time Blocking:
   - Allocate specific time blocks for different activities. This structured approach helps manage time effectively and reduces stress related to deadlines.

12. Use a Planner:
   - Keep a planner to organize tasks, appointments, and deadlines. This visual aid assists in maintaining a sense of control over daily responsibilities.

13. Limit Stimuli:
   - Minimize sensory overload by reducing unnecessary stimuli. Create a calm and organized environment to help manage the challenges of ADHD.

14. Set Realistic Expectations:
   - Set realistic expectations for yourself. Avoid overcommitting and recognize that it's okay to ask for help or delegate tasks.

15. Regular Physical Exercise:
   - Engage in regular physical exercise, as it releases endorphins and helps manage stress. Activities like walking, jogging, or cycling can be effective.

16. Social Support:

- Maintain a strong support network. Sharing concerns and seeking understanding from friends, family, or support groups can be invaluable for stress management.

17. Mindful Eating:
   - Practice mindful eating by savoring each bite and paying attention to the sensory experience. This can contribute to overall well-being and stress reduction.

18. Sleep Hygiene:
   - Prioritize good sleep hygiene by establishing a consistent sleep routine. Quality sleep is essential for managing stress and promoting overall mental health.

Experiment with these relaxation techniques and stress management strategies to discover what works best for you. Consistent practice can contribute to better stress resilience and overall well-being, especially for individuals with ADHD.

Certainly! When considering healthy meals and nutrition for adults with ADHD, it's helpful to focus on nutrient-rich foods that support cognitive function and overall well-being. Here are some key principles:

1. Balanced Diet:
   Ensure a balanced intake of carbohydrates, proteins, and healthy fats. This helps maintain stable blood sugar levels, which can influence mood and concentration.

2. Omega-3 Fatty Acids:
   Include sources of omega-3 fatty acids, such as fatty fish (salmon, mackerel), flaxseeds, and walnuts. Omega-3s are linked to improved cognitive function.

3. Protein-Rich Foods:
Incorporate lean proteins like poultry, eggs, beans, and tofu. Protein helps regulate energy levels and supports the production of neurotransmitters.

4. Complex Carbohydrates:
Opt for whole grains, fruits, and vegetables. These provide a steady release of energy and contain essential vitamins and minerals.

5. Limit Refined Sugars and Processed Foods:
Minimize intake of sugary snacks and processed foods. These can lead to energy crashes and may negatively impact focus and attention.

6. Hydration:
Stay well-hydrated by drinking plenty of water. Dehydration can affect cognitive function and mood.

7. Vitamins and Minerals:
Ensure an adequate intake of vitamins and minerals, especially vitamin B, zinc, and iron. These play a role in cognitive function and mental health.

8. Meal Timing:
Consider smaller, more frequent meals to maintain energy levels throughout the day. This can help prevent energy crashes.

9. Caffeine in Moderation:
While some adults with ADHD find caffeine beneficial, moderation is key. Too much caffeine can lead to jitteriness and interfere with sleep.

10. Mindful Eating:

Encourage mindful eating practices, such as taking time to savor meals. This can promote better digestion and a sense of satisfaction.

Remember, individual responses to foods can vary, so it's essential to observe how specific dietary choices impact personal well-being. Consulting with a healthcare professional or nutritionist can provide personalized guidance based on individual needs and preferences.

Managing ADHD as a couple involves open communication, understanding, and collaborative strategies. Here are some practical tips:

1. Education and Awareness:
   - Both partners should educate themselves about ADHD to understand its impact on daily life.
   - Attend workshops or therapy sessions together to gain insights into ADHD management techniques.

2. Open Communication:
   - Foster open and honest communication about ADHD-related challenges without judgment.
   - Discuss individual needs, concerns, and feelings regularly to maintain a strong connection.

3. Establish Routines and Structure:
   - Create predictable routines and structures to provide stability and reduce anxiety.
   - Use calendars, planners, and reminders to help manage time and tasks effectively.

4. Set Realistic Expectations:
   - Set achievable goals and expectations, recognizing the unique challenges of ADHD.

- Break tasks into smaller, more manageable steps to make them less overwhelming.

5. Teamwork and Collaboration:
   - Work as a team to address daily responsibilities and tasks.
   - Clearly define roles and responsibilities to avoid misunderstandings or frustration.

6. Positive Reinforcement:
   - Celebrate small victories and accomplishments, reinforcing positive behavior.
   - Provide encouragement and support to boost confidence and motivation.

7. Create a Supportive Environment:
   - Foster a supportive environment where both partners feel comfortable expressing their needs.
   - Be patient and understanding during challenging moments, practicing empathy.

8. Professional Assistance:
   - Consider seeking professional help, such as couples therapy or counseling, to navigate ADHD-specific challenges.
   - Involve a healthcare professional in managing medication if it's part of the treatment plan.

9. Self-Care for Both Partners:
   - Prioritize self-care to manage stress and prevent burnout.
   - Encourage each other to engage in activities that promote overall well-being.

10. Flexibility and Adaptability:

- Recognize that flexibility is crucial. Plans may need to be adjusted, and that's okay.
- Adapt strategies as needed and be open to trying new approaches based on ongoing feedback.

Remember, managing ADHD as a couple is an ongoing process that requires patience, understanding, and a collaborative mindset. Regularly reassess and adjust your strategies to create a supportive and thriving relationship.